CANADUH

Other Books by Leland Gregory

CANADUH

Idiots from the Frozen North

LELAND GREGORY

Andrews McMeel
Publishing, LLC
Kansas City • Sydney • London

10 11 12 13 14 RR2 10 9 8 7 6 5 4 3 2 1

ISBN-13: 978-0-7407-9744-6
ISBN-10: 0-7407-9744-1

Library of Congress Control Number: 2010921942

Book design by Holly Ogden
Illustrations by Kevin Brimmer

www.andrewsmcmeel.com

ATTENTION: SCHOOLS AND BUSINESSES

Andrews McMeel books are available at quantity discounts with bulk purchase for educational, business, or sales promotional use. For information, please write to: Special Sales Department, Andrews McMeel Publishing, LLC, 1130 Walnut Street, Kansas City, Missouri 64106.

CANADUH

Jumping into Action

Police in Toronto responded to a 911 call in December 1995 and quickly and easily apprehended two men who had burgled a home. The clumsy criminals' getaway ended abruptly, painfully, and certainly not as planned. The seventeen-year-old sprained his ankle after he jumped off the porch—not too bad, you say, until you find out that he landed on top of his twenty-two-year-old partner. The partner suffered a fractured skull, a broken collarbone and ribs, and a collapsed lung. They were lying in a heap at the bottom of the porch writhing in pain when police arrived—thereby being punished before being sentenced. ✤

A Winnipeg bylaw forbids anyone from striking the sidewalk with a metal object.

We're Number One!

The first person credited with reporting a UFO sighting was a shipbuilder from Nova Scotia named Simeon Perkins. Perkins was also town clerk, county treasurer, commissioner of roads, judge, and, for more than thirty-years, a member of the Nova Scotia House of Assembly, but he is remembered today for his detailed diaries. In one diary entry dated October 12, 1786, Perkins noted

> *A strange story is going that [a] Fleet of Ships have been seen in the air in some part of The Bay of Fundy.... They were said to be seen in New Minas ... by a girl about sunrise and that the girl being frightened called out and two men that were in the house went out and saw the same sight, being 15 ships and a man forward of them with his hand stretched out. They made to the eastward. They were so near, people saw their sides and ports.* 🍁

Doublespeak

Michel Thibodeau, a thirty-four-year-old computer technician with the Canadian House of Commons, sued Air Canada for more than $500,000 because he could not order a 7UP in French. During a flight from Montreal to Ottawa on August 14, 2000, Thibodeau boarded the plane with a friendly "bonjour," and the flight attendant answered in English. More frustrating to Thibodeau was when he tried to order a 7UP in French and was served a Sprite instead. 🍁

In 2007, Thibodeau was in the news once again after filing an official complaint against OC Transpo, Ottawa's public transit company, demanding that bus drivers greet riders with "bonjour" as well as "hello."

What Are Friends For?

A man from Winnipeg purchased a military-style bulletproof vest and wanted to try it out. He asked a friend to shoot him in the chest with a .22 rifle; the vest passed the test. The man then stuffed a phone book under the vest and asked his friend to shoot him with a 12-gauge shotgun. The man survived the blast but suffered cracked ribs. Police have asked the court to withhold gun ownership privileges from the pair for the next five years. ❧

For Whom the Bell Tolls

D id Alexander Graham Bell invent the telephone in Boston or was it really in Brantford, Ontario? The Bell family purchased a ten-and-a-half-acre farm at Tutelo Heights [now Tutela Heights], near Brantford in 1870 when Alexander was twenty-three years old. It was here that Bell first started working on his concept of transmitting sound through wires. Bell received the patent for his telephone in March 1876, and the controversy between Canada and the United States—and, for that matter, the controversy over whether Bell actually invented the telephone in the first place—still rings today. ✦

Michael Wrightman pleaded guilty in Toronto
in February 1993 in the beating death of David Marlatt.
The death occurred after the two got into a fight
over which one had the longer criminal record.

Her Bedside Manner Really Stinks!

A nurse in Ontario has been found guilty of misconduct for purposely passing gas in front of a patient's wife. After the first breaking of wind, the nurse sneered and asked the woman if she "wanted more" before letting another one rip. This isn't the first time the nurse had been reprimanded; she has a history of "demeaning and unprofessional" behavior. In another incident, the registered nurse made the following comment about a bedridden patient who had asked for assistance in getting out of bed: "I don't know why she wants to get up. All she does all day is sit on her ass and spit all over her clothes." 🍁

Put Your Left Foot In . . .

Police on Jedediah Island, British Columbia, were shoe-ins for the most confused police force when a human foot was found still wearing a sock and a size-twelve sneaker. Six days later, on the nearby island of Gabriola, another foot, again wearing a sock and a size-twelve sneaker, was found on the beach. Odd? Yes. But odder still is the fact that they are both right feet and obviously don't belong to the same person. "Finding one foot is like a million to one odds," confirms Royal Canadian Mounted Police spokesman Corporal Garry Cox in an August 31, 2007, *Vancouver Sun* article. "But to find two is crazy. I've heard of dancers with two left feet, but come on." 🍁

An Edmonton law reads "All bicycle riders must signal with the arm before making a turn, and a bicycle rider must keep both hands on the handlebars at all times."

Foot-in-Mouth Disease

An unnamed Manitoba man was found dead in a room at the McLaren Hotel on Main Street in Winnipeg, and officials were baffled as to his cause of death. According to Jim Hull, spokesman for the chief medical examiner, the autopsy report from the September 1998 incident concluded that the man had "choked to death after biting calluses off his feet." 🍁

Up until 1946, there was no such thing as a Canadian citizen; everyone was considered a British subject.

Sharp Knife—Dull Robber

Guy Boissoneault of Sudbury, Ontario, was arrested and charged with robbery of a candy store. Boissoneault entered the store, pulled out an X-Acto knife, and threatened the clerk with it. The clerk, unfazed by the small razor, picked up the phone and called 911 while Boissoneault watched. When the police arrived, the box-cutter bandit was still in the store. Asked why he didn't try to make a break for it, Boissoneault replied, "I can't run too fast." Police were kind enough to give the poor man a lift—to police headquarters. 🍁

"BRIGHTON MAN DIES AFTER DRIVING VEHICLE INTO BURNING HOUSE"

Belleville [Ontario] Intelligencer headline, March 27, 2003

A Shepherd Following the Light

We've all heard the expression "a deer caught in the headlights," but a dog? Firefighters responding to a 911 emergency call in Belleville, Ontario, were faced with a sticky situation. Maggi, a six-month-old husky-shepherd mix, had somehow gotten her head stuck in an empty headlight frame of a truck.

"I've never seen anything like this in my thirteen years with the department," said acting fire captain Rick Lake. The dog couldn't get her head out because there was sharp metal on the inside of the headlight casing. Soaping down the headlight didn't help matters, either, as the dog was, according to Lake, "stuck in there pretty good." A veterinarian sedated the dog and firefighters used an electric saw and pliers to cut her out of the headlight. "This has been a lot better than rescuing a cat from a tree," Lake joked. 🍁

Attention Walmart Shoppers!

According to an article in the July 11, 2006, *Globe and Mail*, a Walmart in Saint-Jean-sur-Richelieu, Quebec, received a bomb threat and quickly evacuated their customers. It turned out to be a false alarm, which was lucky for the store's forty employees, because they were ordered to search through the store to locate the bomb. Had there actually been a bomb, the store would have ended its red-tag sale in favor of a toe-tag sale. 🍁

This Guy Is Nuts

In 2007, police in Guelph, Ontario, were on the lookout for a Caucasian male in his early twenties with a goatee and a large gap between his front teeth. According to a May 28, 2007, Associated Press article, the man hadn't broken any laws nor harmed anyone, but police were nonetheless "concerned."

Six women had complained that the man had approached them and asked for a unique favor—he wanted them to kick him in the groin. According to Sergeant Cate Welsh, "Some of the women obliged him. I would imagine it would be quite painful, but he didn't make a peep, just stood up and went on his way." On two occasions, the man approached on a bicycle. How he peddled away afterward is anyone's guess. 🍁

A twenty-year-old student from Carleton University in Ottawa, Ontario, was engaged in a spitting contest with some of his friends in April 2004. In order to project his spittle the farthest, the young man backed up and took a running start toward the balcony. He fell eleven floors to his death.

Phone It In

The Ontario Federation of Labor in Toronto installed a "bad boss" hotline to gauge labor problems. Great idea, except that soon after the number was announced the system crashed. There were too many calls coming in for it to handle. 🍁

A Rose by Any Other Name

Although Canada officially became a country on July 1, 1867, and is technically known as the Dominion of Canada, several other names for the new country were discussed. Some favorite suggestions were New Britain, Laurentia, and Brittania. Other suggestions were Cabotia, Columbia, Canadia, and Ursalia. When the name "Canada" was officially chosen, Lower and Upper Canada changed their names to Quebec and Ontario respectively. 🍁

"SQUIRREL FIRES REGULAR OCCURRENCE IN CANADIAN BORDER TOWN"

Associated Press headline, July 19, 2005

Air Kiss Off

According to a November 25, 2003, Reuters article, to show their appreciation for a job well done, Air Canada gave each of its one hundred best-performing customer service personnel a coupon worth four dollars, redeemable only at restaurants owned by its in-flight food service contractor. Giving an employee a coupon for airline food—isn't that more like a punishment than a gift?

Urine Trouble Now

The Gainers meatpacking plant in Edmonton is having a, well, pissing contest with the local union. The union can't hold its temper, or its water, over a ruling that workers have to pay for their bathroom breaks. The Alberta arbitration board upheld the Gainers regulation that docks the pay of workers who go to the bathroom outside of their scheduled breaks, because refusing to pay employees who are not actually on the job [but in the bathroom or on the phone] doesn't violate the collective agreement between the union and the plant. Representatives of Gainers stated that the policy was put into place because workers were abusing bathroom breaks. [Either that or they're all incontinent.] 🍁

They Put the Nut in Doughnut

Nick Skalkos was celebrating his twenty-fifth birthday with his girlfriend, Sarah LeRiche, and twenty of his friends in a doughnut shop in Kitchener, Ontario. Dressed in jeans and running shoes, Nick casually told Sarah that he loved her. The jelly-filled doughnuts must have gone to his head because when a friend asked when they were going to get married, Nick, with a glazed look in his eyes, surprised everyone. He grabbed his honey bun and asked one of their guests, the Reverend Frank Quinto, if he would perform the marriage ceremony right then. Even though the minister said it was the "weirdest wedding" he's ever been to, it was perfectly legal.

I wonder if the guests threw sprinkles instead of rice. 🍁

Oh, Oh, Oh, Canada

A survey conducted in September 2005 by JWT Worldwide, a New York–based ad agency, asked 2,126 English-speaking men and women in the United States, Great Britain, Canada, and the Netherlands a series of questions regarding sex. Canada ranks number one in terms of female sexual satisfaction. But 43 percent of the Canadian women said sex is overrated, and 29 percent of the men agreed with the statement. 🍁

An aboriginal Manitoba woman accused an Extra Foods store of racial profiling after they refused to sell her hairspray. According to a December 3, 2002, CBC News report, the owners might have feared that the woman wanted only to drink it.

He Said, She Said

In 2000, Susan Macintosh moved in with her now common-law husband, Ray Lindley. Soon the couple celebrated the birth of their first child and seemed to be the perfect little family. But bad news struck their household in January 2003 when Ray told Susan he had cancer and needed to go to Montreal for treatment. Then things got worse. Ray didn't have cancer, but what he did have he had removed: Ray had a sex-change operation. When Ray—now known as Cara-Anne—returned, Susan was aghast at seeing his feminine side and decided to sever their relationship.

In mid-2004, Cara-Anne visited Susan at her home, and possibly having forgotten to take her hormone pills, became enraged and struck her twenty times with a tire iron. Susan survived the attack but required major reconstructive surgery. [Not as reconstructive as Cara-Anne's, however.] Cara-Anne was sentenced to five years in prison for the assault. ❧

Taken for a Ride

The man's eyes darted around the bank as he reached into his pocket and pulled out the crumpled hold-up note. The teller at the Canadian Imperial Bank of Commerce in Gatineau, Quebec, accepted the note and unfolded it, but she wasn't able to read it. The note was written in English and the teller understood only French. She left the robber standing there and took the note to other tellers for assistance.

The man began to feel uneasy as a crowd gathered around the teller to help her translate the note. Panic got the best of him, and he dashed out of the bank into his getaway car—a taxi he had waiting around the corner. He gave the driver instructions to take him to downtown Ottawa and sat back in the cab to calm his nerves.

Once in the city, the man thought he would be able to go through with the robbery again and told the driver to turn the car around and head back to Gatineau. The driver looked at the haggard man sitting in the backseat and asked if he had enough money to pay the fare. Checking his pockets, the man admitted he was short of cash and couldn't pay the meter. The driver slammed on the brakes, got out of his car, and called the police.

The man was arrested and charged with armed robbery in connection with the failed attempt at the bank. He was later charged with a second count of armed robbery involving a Bank of Nova Scotia in Gatineau. Said Sergeant Richard Longpre of the Gatineau police, "It wasn't such a smooth job by that guy."

IT'S A LIVING
PART I

In 2009, as part of the 115th Labour Day celebration, Ancestry.ca put together a list of some of the strangest jobs in the history of Canada from 1851 to 1916—and there are no firefighters, ballerinas, or police officers in this bunch.

LUNATIC KEEPER. According to the 1901 census, forty-eight-year-old John Corbett from Saint John, New Brunswick, has the distinction of being Canada's only official lunatic keeper.

CRIMINAL. When asked for his occupation on the 1901 census, nineteen-year-old John Middleton from Algoma, Ontario, was honest and wrote, "Criminal."

IDIOT. Although this doesn't qualify as an occupation [unless your job is to write books like this one], the 1901 census listed three people as idiots, meaning they were patients in asylums.

BEGGAR. Between 1851 and 1916, Canada had nearly forty people officially claiming to be professional beggars. One was twenty-five-year-old Mary Munroe of Yarmouth, Nova Scotia.

What Will the Neighbors Think?

Two Canadian astronomers beamed a twenty-three-page message into outer space in the hope that it would help alien life forms understand the human race and our level of intelligence. But in June 1999, a month after the signal was sent, the astronomers admitted they had made a mistake. A portion of the message to show how humans have evolved in their understanding of mathematics used two different "equals to" symbols. The Dutch researcher who originally uncovered the mistake was disheartened because he believes now aliens will think that earthlings are "a sloppy species." 🍁

According to a September 30, 2002, article in the *Globe and Mail*, at her trial for harsh disciplining of children at her commune, former nun Lucille Poulin of Charlottetown, Prince Edward Island, testified that "It isn't easy, but God said to [beat them]."

These Guys Are Nuts

The government of Ontario came under considerable criticism, according to a March 20, 2003, CBC News report, after it gave a $150,000 grant to researchers at Laurentian University. The grant helped fund a project whose purpose was to study how wildlife adapts to the environment by examining, in detail, the sex drives of squirrels. 🍁

What Does the Gas Pedal Do?

Police thought the driver of an armored truck in Edmonton was trying to signal them for help by repeatedly opening and closing the truck's door. Calling for backup, the original officer and five other patrol cars pulled the armored car over to find out the true nature of the problem. It turned out there wasn't an emergency; the driver was simply trying to fan fresh air into the cab after his partner had passed gas. 🍁

According to a May 2, 2002, article in the *National Post,* Michel Lariviere, a psychologist for Correctional Services of Canada, issued a paper that concluded that rehabilitation efforts are hindered because most guards don't respect inmates.

The Flight of the Living Dead

You never know who you'll wind up sitting next to on a crowded airplane: the talkative type, the person who's afraid of flying, the airsick passenger, or worse. Well, one Canadian family complained to Continental Airlines because they were stuck with the worst kind of passenger—a dead one. After a sick passenger, hooked up to IVs and oxygen, foamed at the mouth and died during an April 2001 flight across the Pacific, he was kept in his seat for the duration of the five-hour flight. 🍁

Never a Train Shall Meet

An emergency 911 call came into the Oshawa, Ontario, 911 center: A man had been run over by a train. Police and an ambulance crew arrived at the scene expecting to find the shattered body of some poor soul. They talked with the train's engineer to get the complete story. Apparently the man had staggered out of a bar earlier that night and passed out between a set of train tracks.

The train's engineer had slammed on the emergency brakes when he saw the man but was unable to stop the train in time. In horror, the engineer watched as the train ran over the man's body. Paramedics found the man easily. He was lying on the ground a little farther down the tracks—sound asleep. When he was awakened, the man didn't know what had happened and didn't realize how close he had come to death. Investigators said the fact that he was so out of it had probably saved his life, because he didn't move when the train passed over his body. "If he had woken up and sat up he would have been in trouble," said Sergeant Jim Grimley of the Durham Regional Police Service. And they say alcohol has no redeeming benefits. ❦

Stowaway We Go!

As a ship left Vancouver, a thirty-six-year-old man from Nanaimo, British Columbia, tried to stow away—the hard way. The man positioned himself on a bridge, knowing the ship would pass underneath him. He had a bungee cord firmly tied around his waist, and he planned to jump down onto the ship, cut the cord, and gain a free cruise. As soon as the ship was in position, the man leaped from the bridge but didn't properly calculate the weight of his body, the distance of the fall, or the tension of the cord.

Instead of gracefully stopping a few feet above the deck, the man slammed onto the ship's tennis court and then bounced back up. On his way back down he crashed into the railing of the stern and was left dangling above the water like a yo-yo. He finally splashed into the water, where the crew of a passing boat rescued him. Life has its little ups and downs, but this guy had them all in one day. ❦

Insurance Rider

Employees of the Coachman Insurance Company in Toronto watched as the driver of a 1990 Pontiac Bonneville jumped curbs, crashed into another car, and knocked over a brick wall in the company parking lot. The driver of the car leaped out, fell to his knees, and threw his hands up as in prayer.

He yelled, "I didn't do it, honest to God I didn't do it. Someone hit me," to Cynthia Cormier, the owner of a car he had damaged. What was embarrassing about the incident is that the driver's father was inside the insurance company collecting a check for a prior accident involving the same car, which had been written off as totaled and shouldn't have been on the road. The other embarrassing element was that the driver was the man's ten-year-old son. The boy wasn't charged because of his age, but his father is responsible for the $8,000 in damages he caused. ❦

Head and Shoulders

In May 2006, Shee Theng of Edmonton was sentenced to nine months of community service for partially scalping his then-girlfriend. Theng told the judge that the scalping was an accident as he was merely trying to "style" her hair with a power drill. Shee convinced the judge that he had learned about the barbaric barbering technique from a TV infomercial and knew it was a bad idea as he had screwed up his own hair with the drill a bit earlier. 🍁

Five-Finger Discount

Police in West Vancouver, British Columbia, arrested multimillionaire Eugene Mah and his son Avery on charges of theft. But we're not talking about a white collar/Enron-type crime; we're talking about petty theft. The rich father-and-son team [worth an estimated $13 million] stole hundreds of items from their upscale neighborhood, including garbage cans, concrete lawn decorations, and even government recycling boxes, which they stored at their own elegant home. According to an April 26, 2001, Canadian Press article, the Mahs also stole their neighbor's welcome mat—and every one of the fourteen welcome mats the family purchased as replacements. 🍁

No Pain, No Gain

A pregnant woman from Hamilton, Ontario, sued her doctors and McMaster Hospital for $2.4 million because she had pain while giving birth. She claimed that her doctors had promised her birth would be "so pain-free, she could knit or read a book during the procedure." But the pain was so traumatizing, the woman testified, that she had "intrusive thoughts"—believing, for example, that the hospital had secretly called her dentist and asked him to make sure "I have as much pain as possible during dental treatment." The woman, whose husband happens to be a physician at McMaster [wink, wink], said she filed the suit not for the money but "to make sure this doesn't happen to anyone else." 🍁

An unnamed forty-four-year-old man arrested in connection with a marijuana-growing scheme skipped out of his court appearance in April 2007 and was arrested in December of that year when he applied for a job at the county jail.

Front-End Suspensi..

A man on the run from the law tried to evade police by crawling under a parked tractor-trailer in Toronto in March 2006. But the hide-and-seek half-wit picked the wrong truck, because, before he could crawl out, the truck started up and headed down Highway 401 with the suspect hanging on underneath.

A passing motorist noticed the driver was hauling more than he suspected and called police. Authorities had to stop traffic on the busy highway and arrested the suspended suspected car thief. "I'm amazed that this young man is still alive, to be honest with you," Ontario provincial police constable Joel Doiron said. 🍁

Never a Twain Shall Meet

Matt Brownlee, considered a recidivist drunk driver, was acquitted of criminal DUI charges in Ottawa according to a March 28, 2006, report from the Canadian Broadcasting Corporation. Psychiatrists concluded that the thirty-three-year-old man's latest accident stemmed from a brain injury he sustained in a 1996 accident, in which he believed that Shania Twain was helping him drive the car. [Brownlee was diagnosed with a disorder that makes him believe he is in telepathic communication with celebrities.] ✺

It's the Great Pumpkin!

What better way to celebrate Thanksgiving than by racing on Pesaquid Lake in a half-pumpkin? But that's just what the annual Windsor-West Hants Pumpkin Regatta held in Windsor, Nova Scotia, is all about. Nearly ten thousand spectators watch fifty contestants paddle pumpkins or even race motorized pumpkins in the quest for pumpkin supremacy. In the 2008 race, Anthony Cook won the paddling event in his giant hollowed-out pumpkin painted to resemble a soccer ball, while Dani Rippey won first place in the motorized class. 🍁

In 2006, domestic diva
Martha Stewart attempted to
compete in the pumpkin race, but
she was originally denied entry
because Canadian immigration
officials bar ex-convicts from
entering the country (Stewart
served time for lying to feds about
a stock sale). Eventually she got
the green light to participate, but
bad weather grounded her in
an airport in Maine.

The Artsy Bunch

An art exhibit in Halifax consisted of a regular banana placed on one of the presenting gallery's windowsills. Each day the artist, Michael Fernandes, would replace the old banana with a newer, greener banana and eat the one he removed. Fernandes placed an asking price on the banana at $2,500 [reduced from the original $15,000], and, believe it or not, he received two offers.

According to a July 2, 2008, article in the *Globe and Mail*, gallery co-owner Victoria Page felt obligated to make sure the bidders really knew what they were getting for their money: "It's a banana; you understand that it's a banana?" It just proves that some art still has appeal. ✿

Cracked Crystal Ball

The school board in Barrie, Ontario, alerted the Children's Aid Society to suspected sexual abuse of an autistic eleven-year-old girl named Victoria. Upon investigation, the girl's mom found out that the suspicion stemmed from a teaching assistant who said her psychic had revealed to her that a twenty-something-year-old man was abusing a girl with a "V" in her name. Victoria's mother removed the girl from the public school system, according to a June 19, 2008, article in the *National Post*, because "They might want to take out a Ouija board or hold a séance." ❦

A Prime Minister in His Prime

The first prime minister of Canada, Sir John Alexander Macdonald [1815–91], is remembered for three things: being the first prime minister, his sharp wit, and his alcoholism. One of the most popular stories about Macdonald concerned a debate in which he was involved where he was so drunk that he vomited on stage.

His opponent directed the audience's attention to Macdonald and shouted, "Is this the man you want running your country? A drunk!"

Collecting himself, Macdonald replied, "I get sick . . . not because of drink [but because] I am forced to listen to the ranting of my honorable opponent." 🍁

Three's Company

According to a June 21, 2007, article in the *Toronto Star*, two elderly male residents at a Toronto nursing home got into an altercation over a woman that resulted in one death. A seventy-nine-year-old man had taken up with a female resident at the home, believing her to be his wife. This angered a sixty-nine-year-old man who thought the woman was *his* wife, and he kicked the other resident, causing him to fall and fatally hit his head. The woman in question was married to neither of the men. All three of the residents suffered from Alzheimer's disease. 🍁

You're from where?
How about Medicine Hat,
Alberta; Cape Spear, New
Brunswick; Come by Chance,
Newfoundland and Labrador;
Joe Batt's Arm, Newfoundland
and Labrador; Heart's Content,
Newfoundland and Labrador;
Hearts' Desire, Newfoundland
and Labrador; or Starvation Cove
in Nunavut?

Crime Doesn't Pay Much

Twenty-three-year-old Christopher Emmorey walked into a Peterborough, Ontario, bank and demanded $2,000 from the teller. The teller told Emmorey that she could give him only $200 and that he must pay a $5 fee because he wasn't a regular customer; Emmorey agreed. He took the $195 and, according to a May 25, 2007, article in the *Peterborough Examiner*, walked out of the bank. He was arrested a short time later. 🍁

Killing the Pain

Police pulled over fifty-one-year-old Benoit Derosiers, who was so inebriated that he could barely speak and had trouble standing, and arrested him for DUI. But when Derosiers appeared before the provincial court in Sudbury, Ontario, he convinced the judge that he had a "legal necessity" for driving while intoxicated.

According to an April 18, 2007, *Globe and Mail* article, Derosiers explained to the judge that he had just attempted suicide and needed to drive himself, in his intoxicated state, to the nearest hospital because he feared that he would attempt to kill himself again if he didn't. The judge agreed with Derosiers's decision, and he was released. 🍁

"TASER SHOCK TRIGGERS FIRE IN MAN'S PANTS"

Hamilton [Ontario] Spectator headline, April 19, 2008

Just Chillin'

A teenage boy from Hamilton, Ontario, was discovered, nearly naked, hanging onto a rope and dangling upside down from the side of a bridge on an exceptionally cold [-4°F, -20°C] night. After he was rescued by some partygoers who had just left a nearby home, the fifteen-year-old boy confessed that he had been tobogganing alone around 8 p.m. and got the idea to spray graffiti on the side of the bridge when things turned bad. According to a February 15, 2007, article in the *Hamilton Spectator*, the teen got tangled in the rope and, while he was squirming to free himself, he lost some of his clothing. 🍁

Insert Your Face Here . . .

"The Fun Guide" is a brochure published by the city of Toronto showing, of course, fun things to do around the city. The family on the front of the cover is described as a family of "indeterminate ethnic background"—the family "looks maybe Latino," said city spokesman Kevin Sack. In order for the family to be more "inclusive," said a July 2009 article in the *National Post*, the city had the printer paste the face of a black man over the father figure. "You won't find a more inclusive organization than us," Sack said. He's right. It's the best Photoshopped family one could make. 🍁

Local Boy Makes Good

A lvin "Creepy" Karpis was born Alvin Francis Karpowicz in Montreal, Quebec, on August 10, 1907. Karpis received the nickname "Creepy" because of his sinister smile. A notorious gangster known for his affiliation with the Barker gang in the 1930s, he was arrested on May 1, 1936, and sentenced to life imprisonment. He holds the title for the longest sentence served at Alcatraz [August 1936 to April 1962] and was one of the few prisoners who never attempted to escape. Karpis was released on parole in 1969 and deported to Canada, where he found it difficult to obtain a Canadian passport because he had had his fingerprints surgically removed in 1934. ♦

On November 21, 2008, the Canadian Press reported that twenty-one-year-old Louise Light was not injured when she smashed her car into guideposts in Woodstock, Ontario, but she did wind up being covered in milk—the woman had been eating cereal from a bowl while driving.

Man-to-Man

In real estate the mantra is "Location, location, location." The same can be said of perpetrating a crime. One robber accosted a woman in downtown Edmonton in July 2009 and got away with her purse and laptop computer. But in the same location was Kitwana Jones, a defensive end for the Edmonton Eskimos of the Canadian Football League, who gave chase. Soon the six-foot-tall, 227-pound football player had put some defensive pressure on the thief and brought him down. The thief was charged with robbery. 🍁

Stream of Consciousness

The *National Post* newspaper reported in September 1999 that the automatic-flush toilets at the University of Toronto Athletic Centre health club weren't functioning properly. According to a health club official, there wasn't enough time for them to work. The toilets required a minimum of nine seconds to reset the flushing trigger, and since the men who use the urinals were usually naked, there was no time spent zipping and unzipping. 🍁

"MAN CHARGED FOR TRYING TO MACGYVER PROPANE TANK TO CAR ENGINE"

London [Ontario] Free Press headline, February 15, 2007

Excuses, Excuses

A traffic officer in eastern Ontario gave a speeding ticket to a tourist from Switzerland, according to a September 7, 2006, Associated Press article. The speeding Swiss told the officer the reason he felt obligated to speed was because, unlike in his country, there were no goats to wander out onto the road. 🍁

In 2005, Professor Mary Valentich of the University of Calgary in Alberta started a study as to why some female fans expose their breasts at hockey games while others don't.

The Jerky Boys

The Royal Canadian Mounted Police in Saskatchewan admitted they'll probably never find the contents of a locked delivery truck that was vandalized and robbed in Saskatoon in February 2007. The news, and the truck's contents, are hard to swallow. The thieves caused more than $3,000 worth of damage to the truck and got away with approximately $500 worth of dried meat products, including a case of beef sticks, a case of pepperoni sticks, and a case of beef jerky. 🍁

That's What Friends Are For?

An unnamed man from Val-des-Monts, Quebec, was smoking crack with his housemates when he suffered a seizure, which apparently startled not only the man's friends but also his pit bull terrier. The dog attacked the forty-one-year-old man and bit him under the ear. One of the other crackheads jumped up, grabbed a baseball bat, and took a swing at the dog—but missed. He cracked the attacked crackhead in the face by mistake. The injured man was taken to a hospital where a plastic bag containing ten grams of crack was found in his crack. He was charged with possession of drugs with intent to sale and owning an illegal breed of dog. 🍁

Put One Big Foot in Front of the Other

C anadian member of Parliament Mike Lake is adamant about protecting an endangered species, but not just any endangered species: He wants to protect Sasquatch, the legendary hairy manlike beast said to roam the wilderness of British Columbia and other parts of North America, and known by dozens of other names, such as Big Foot or Yeti.

Lake presented a petition signed by five hundred of his constituents asking "to establish immediate, comprehensive legislation to effect immediate protection of Bigfoot." According to a May 3, 2007, article in the *Vancouver Province,* Lake is fighting hard to have Sasquatch protected under Canada's Species at Risk Act. 🍁

A man armed with a bottle of toilet cleaner robbed a shopkeeper in Norwich, Ontario.

Out-of-This-World Technology

C limate change is the number one problem facing the world today," said Paul Hellyer, an eighty-three-year-old former Canadian defense minister. "We need to persuade governments to come clean on what they know." And what exactly is this secret technology of which Hellyer is speaking? Alien technology, of course, according to a February 28, 2007, article in the *Ottawa Citizen*. Hellyer insists that governments have obviously picked up a multitude of advanced technologies from various UFO crash sites that "could be a way to save our planet." 🍁

Final Stump Speech

R obert Case complained to the Essex Region Conservation Authority for several years about a dangerous tree stump in Lake Saint Clair near his home in Lakeshore, Ontario. Case claimed the stump was dangerous to snowmobilers who might not see the stump and crash into it, but the ERCA did nothing since, according to a spokesman, "The beds of the Great Lakes are the responsibility of the provincial government."

According to a February 5, 2007, article in the *Windsor Star*, Case was snowmobiling late at night on the frozen lake at speeds of 70 kph [45 mph] when he struck the stump he had been complaining about and was "ejected from the snowmobile quite a distance," a police spokesman said, killing him instantly. Case's wife, Grace, is considering suing the ERCA, claiming her husband "knew what he was doing. He wasn't stupid." 🍁

Put a Sock in It

The *National Post* published a lengthy article on November 11, 2006, about an unnamed forty-one-year-old engineer from suburban Toronto who has collected [and worn] nearly eight hundred pairs of sports socks over the past fifteen years. Although he accumulated nearly half of his collection from professional athletes, he swears he doesn't have a sock fetish, preferring to call himself a "custodian of history." However, the sock fancier says he has fielded hundreds of inquiries from legitimate foot and sock fetishists and continues to keep his collection a secret from his wife. 🍁

Enough Is Too Much

I want to help people who are suffering without food," said eight-year-old Stephanie Templeton, a third grader at Derrydown Public School in North York, Ontario. "We have lots of food and it makes me feel good to give it to people." But apparently the girl brought in too much food, claimed her teacher, and she was told to take most of it back home. "The teacher said she was showing up the other kids," said Stephanie's father, Frank, who complained to the school's principal, Yvonne Castello. The principal agreed with the teacher's feelings but overrode her decision and allowed Stephanie to contribute as much food as she wanted. Not surprisingly, the food drive for that year [2006] was the most successful the school has held. ❧

What Are the Odds?

In October 2006, the Canadian Broadcasting Company profiled the winners of the Ontario lottery from 1999 to 2006 and found out that the biggest winners were ... ticket sellers and others employed in the lottery system. The CBC report, which aired on the show *The Fifth Estate,* showed that more retailers were winning instead of the customers; 214 "insiders" have won $50,000 or more.

Jeffrey Rosenthal, a statistician at the University of Toronto, said the odds of this many retailers winning are one in a trillion, trillion, trillion, trillion—that's a one followed by forty-eight zeroes. The odds that you'll be hit by lightning in the next year are one in five million, said Rosenthal, whose book *Struck by Lightning: The Curious World of Probabilities* also includes the chances that you'll be killed in your next vehicle trip: one in seven million. ✦

The Story of the Three Little Pigs

Lucette Saint Louis, a sixty-six-year-old woman from Corbeil, Ontario, was trying to corral three escaped pigs, belonging to her son, Marc, when one of them ran out onto the road. Before Saint Louis could do anything about it, a passing car struck the 180-pound pig, throwing it into the air. The pig slammed into Saint Louis, breaking her leg in two places. "Well, at least," she said, "I can tell my grandchildren that pigs really do fly." 🍁

A grocery story robbery in Calgary was hindered because of two things: 1) the robber's only weapon was an ordinary manual can opener, and 2) during the attempted getaway the sixteen-month-old baby of the robber's girlfriend kept falling out of the stroller.

Sex!
Now That I've Got
Your Attention . . .

From now on you'll find no more sex in Middlesex. Well, only when it comes to the e-mail world, that is. Spam filters have been a problem with the Ontario county for some time now—blocking some e-mails because the word "sex" is flagged. So the county has decided to get a sex change. It has bought a new domain name that ends with @mdlsx.ca, replacing their old addresses ending in @county.middlesex.on.ca, which, said chief administrative officer Bill Rayburn, "is a mouthful." 🍁

The Seeds of a Crime

I t is a peculiar item to steal," said Constable Stephen Senuita, a spokesman for the Portage la Prairie detachment of the Royal Canadian Mounted Police. "This is the first instance of this type of property being stolen that I can think of." Constable Senuita was referring to a tank containing $15,000 worth of bull semen that was stolen from a property in the Rural Municipality of North Norfolk west of Winnipeg on March 9, 2009.

Bob Wotton, an artificial insemination technician and distributor based in MacGregor, about 120 kilometers [75 miles] west of Winnipeg, said $15,000 worth "would be a lot of semen." He also stated that it would be difficult to resell the semen because buyers would be curious where it came from. 🍁

That Sinking Feeling

In September 1992, twenty-two-year-old David Wayne Godin was returning from his bachelor stag party when he lost control of his vehicle and plunged into a lake near Dartmouth, Nova Scotia. Authorities determined that Godin might not have drowned had it not been for a wacky party gift his friends had attached to his leg—an actual ball and chain. If they would have given him a battle-ax he might have been able to cut his way out of his sinking car. 🍁

According to an August 5, 2003, article in the *Toronto Star,* a twenty-nine-year-old man caused a traffic jam after stopping his vehicle in the passing lane on the highway because "he was too nervous to drive in the rain."

What's in a Name?

According to a February 3, 2006, CBC News report, James Clifford Hanna, from the Yukon Territory, argued in court that "James Clifford Hanna" was simply a name involuntarily given to him at birth. He argued that he was never given the opportunity to officially accept the name and therefore he shouldn't be obligated to pay James Clifford Hanna's taxes. A judge told James Clifford Hanna that he is responsible for James Clifford Hanna's actions. 🍁

A Professor with No Class

According to a January 27, 2006, article in the *Globe and Mail*, University of Prince Edward Island history professor David Weale offered a grade of B-minus to students in his overcrowded class if they would just go away. The administration discovered that twenty of the ninety-five students in Weale's class accepted the offer. Weale, who had retired but came back to teach that single course, soon re-retired. 🍁

Us Doesn't Mean You

In 1880, Canada created the Department of Indian Affairs to control the assets, culture, and religion of the First Nation Canadians. The Indian Act made it very clear to whom they were referring: "The term person means an individual other than an Indian." 🍁

Got Milk?

A $9,000 grant by the Canada Council for the Arts enraged Conservative legislators in Ottawa because the money went to controversial performance artist Jess Dobkin. Dobkin's previous work included *The Two Boobs,* a puppet show that featured painted faces on her breasts that moved by strings attached to her nipples. According to a June 16, 2006, Canadian Press article, the legislators were outraged because the money went for Dobkin's "Lactation Station Breast Milk Bar," allowing people to sample human breast milk in a setting similar to a wine tasting. 🍁

Hey Guys, Watch This!

C ory McKinnon of London, Ontario, told his friend he
was bored and needed "something to do." So the twenty-
two-year-old attempted to scale down the side of his high-
rise apartment complex, jumping from balcony to balcony.
According to a January 17, 2001, *National Post* article, he lost his
grip when he got back to his balcony and fell seven floors to his
death. ❀

In 1922, future Canadian prime minister Lester Bowles
Pearson earned a position on Britain's Olympic hockey team.
Today, an award bearing his name is given to the best
hockey player voted on by members of the
National Hockey League Players' Association.

The Truth Is Out There

In April 1999, thirty-four-year-old Rene Joly filed a lawsuit in Toronto against several drugstore chains and the Honorable Art Eggleton, PC, MP, who was the defense minister at the time, charging that they had conspired to kill him. Joly claimed several attempts had been made on his life, that his prescriptions were poisoned, and that a microchip had been implanted in his brain. He told reporters in May that since he had been cloned using materials recovered from NASA missions, "Genetically speaking, I'm a Martian, yes." Although the college-educated Joly eloquently presented his case, one defense lawyer remarked that Joly "has watched too many episodes of *The X-Files*." ◆

A Stable Relationship

With the enactment of the Civil Marriage Act on July 20, 2005, Canada became the fourth country in the world and the first country in the Americas to legalize same-sex marriage nationwide. It garnered unbridled approval from two members of the Royal Canadian Mounted Police when they decided to get married. Constable Jason Tree and Constable David Connors work in different divisions of the RCMP, according to a June 7, 2006, article in the *Seattle Times*, but have known each other since college. Gives a whole different meaning to "Mounted Police" now, doesn't it? 🍁

IT'S A LIVING
PART II

In 2009, as part of the 115th Labour Day celebration, Ancestry. ca put together a list of some of the strangest jobs in the history of Canada from 1851 to 1916. Here are some more weird careers.

WITCH. In the 1881 census, forty-eight-year-old John Quinn of Gaspé, Quebec, is listed as a "witch."

MONSTER. Forty-two-year-old Robert Hosking of Huron County, Ontario, a husband and father of four, listed his occupation as "monster" in the 1901 census.

PIG NURSE. Twenty-six-year-old Toronto resident Mary Brown is listed in the 1901 census as a "pig nurse." I'm not sure what this position entails: It's either a specialty in the field of veterinary medicine or a very ugly woman.

I've Got You Under My Spell

In 2006, Brad Wall of the Saskatchewan Party wanted to be the Canadian province's new premier but wound up spending most of his time explaining why the party makes so many spelling errors. In different campaign publications, "Saskatchewan" was spelled "Saskatchwan" and "Saskatcheawn," and a press release used the creative spelling of "goverment." In a video, the last name of Lorne Calvert, the current premier, was spelled "Clavert." In another instance, the party referred to the "Saskatchean Libeals" when they meant Saskatchewan Liberals.

Wall defended his campaign's spelling snafus by claiming there are "instances when all the proofreading in the world still doesn't catch everything." That's the trut. 🍁

Father and Son Reunion

A partygoer at a New Year's Eve bash in Nanaimo, British Columbia, got out of control, drunkenly tried to kiss one of the female attendees, and started dancing around, wearing nothing but a leopard-print thong. Police were called, and the man tried to clonk one of the officers with a partly full soda bottle before he was arrested for assault. It was highly embarrassing for the man who was throwing the party because the obnoxious guest was his own sixty-two-year-old father, Alan Bethell.

Bethell's lawyer blamed his antics on the fact that he had mixed prescription medicine with alcohol and was simply trying "to recapture his youth" and "be a teenager again." According to an April 12, 2006, article in the *Victoria Times Colonist*, Bethell was fined $805. He was forgiven by his wife but hasn't made up with his son. 🍁

People Eat Baby Corn, Don't They?

In early May 2006, the electronic signs on at least five GO Transit train cars in Toronto flashed this message about the prime minister every three seconds: "Stephen Harper Eats Babies. Stephen Harper Eats Babies. Stephen Harper Eats Babies." A transit spokesman explained it wasn't a news update; it was the work of a hacker who had reprogrammed the signs.

Gerry Nicholls, vice president of the National Citizens Coalition, once headed by Harper, said he saw one of the flashing messages, but that it wasn't true. "I worked with Stephen Harper for five years," Nicholls said, "and never once did he in that time eat a baby." 🍁

Sir William Pearce Howland (1811–1907) is distinguished as the only Father of Confederation born in the United States.

A Newspaper Connoisseur

E ven with the advent of electronic media some people claim they'll never give up printed newspapers. One woman who says she'll never lose her taste for newsprint is a seventy-year-old woman identified only as Maggie. She told the *Edmonton Sun* on September 5, 2007, that the *Sun* is literally part of her daily diet: She eats it.

"I can't explain it," said Maggie, who said she has torn the newspaper into strips and devoured them every day for the past seven years. She admitted to her reading and eating disorder after she experienced a blockage of her esophagus, and doctors removed a ball of paper. Although eating newspapers could pose a chocking hazard, doctors cited by the *Sun* said that newspaper consumption is not unhealthy. 🍁

This Is a Public Service Announcement

According to a January 29, 2009, CTV report, police officers in Airdrie, Alberta, responded to a call of concern from the Ralph McCall Elementary School. A man was standing in the schoolyard with a portable loudspeaker directed toward a group of kids on the playground, saying, "Girls in the field, come over to my truck. Come pet my dog." When several adults approached him, he quickly jumped in his truck and drove away. 🍁

Fred Rose holds the distinction of being the only Communist ever elected (1943) to the Canadian Parliament.

Point of Order

During the November 2008 rape trail of an Edmonton bus driver, the victim took the stand and was asked by the prosecutor to identify her attacker in the courtroom. The woman adjusted her glasses and glanced around the room and dramatically pointed to a man standing near the back of the courtroom, a CBC reporter who had nothing to do with the rape. Owing to the overwhelming evidence against her attacker the judge allowed the woman to try again. This time she focused her attention, and her finger, on the guilty party. ❦

From No Charge to Charged

A fifty-three-year-old Vernon, British Columbia, man and his twenty-year-old partner were arrested and charged with robbing a Canadian Imperial Bank of Commerce in January 2008. The older man had left his companion in the getaway car while he went in to rob the bank. When he came out with the loot they discovered that the battery was dead because the younger associate had been listening to the radio with the engine off. They were easily apprehended at another bank nearby because the CIBC bank is located in the same building as a RCMP station. 🍁

In September 2003, the Manitoba government announced it was ordering forty thousand condoms of "assorted flavors," such as "strawberry, banana, and vanilla," for prisoners in its ten jails. According to a September 15, 2003, article in the *Winnipeg Free Press,* the number of condoms was reduced after the information became public.

Highway Robbery

In Ottawa, red-light enforcement cameras, which detect vehicles that cross intersections during red traffic lights, aren't just catching private citizens; they're also catching public servants. Police, firefighters, and paramedics are required by law to stop at all red lights before proceeding, even if they are running emergency services. Rolling stops are illegal. The city won't give any violator slack, and every offender gets a $180 ticket. The city has garnered more than $11,000 from emergency agencies since the red-light enforcement cameras came into use. 🍁

Two of the thirty-six Fathers of Confederation had the exact same name: John Hamilton Gray. One was from New Brunswick; the other from Prince Edward Island.

A Violent Newscast

A husband and wife in Surrey, British Columbia, were watching the news when a fight broke out—between the two of them. Words flew and soon fists did, too. The husband slapped his wife twice across the back of her head, and she quickly retaliated by smashing a glass jar over his. The RCMP were called to the residence and discovered the cause of the fight.

"The violence on the news was disconcerting to the woman," said police sergeant Roger Morrow, in an April 16, 2009, *Vancouver Sun* article. The husband was arrested. The couple's three children slept soundly during the entire ordeal. 🍁

A Roll in the Trash

A report of "suspicious persons" was called into police headquarters in Saanich, British Columbia, and an officer was dispatched to investigate. When he arrived at the location it appeared deserted, but then the officer heard noise from inside a trash Dumpster. He peered inside and found a man and woman "intertwined" among the rubbish and "oblivious to his presence." According to an April 24, 2009, article in the *Victoria Times Colonist*, the thirty-year-old woman was released but her twenty-six-year-old companion was arrested on an unrelated warrant. 🍁

In 1867, federal politicians earned six dollars a day (still too much if you ask most people).

Drive-By Reasoning

I f you're pulled over in your car for driving on a restricted license and having too many passengers in your car, what excuse can you use? Well, Cindy June Dilts of Comox Valley, British Columbia, came up with a good one: She said she was the only sober one in the group. According to a July 2009 article in the *Comox Valley Echo*, a sympathetic judge, Peter Doherty, appreciated her logic but still sentenced her to fourteen days in jail and a $300 fine. 🍁

Wing Attack Plan "R"

Colonel James "Buster" Sutherland Brown, Canadian director of military operations and intelligence, created Defense Scheme No. 1 at Canadian army headquarters in 1921. The plan was basically a preemptive invasion of the United States in which Canadian troops would immediately be deployed to seize Seattle, Washington; Great Falls, Montana; Minneapolis, Minnesota; and Albany, New York, in a surprise attack. The plan seems a little crazy until one learns that the United States drafted American War Plan Red, a 1930s plan to invade Canada. 🍁

The *Thunder Bay Chronicle Journal* reported on March 4, 2006, that twenty-five-year-old Nathan Myles was sentenced to three years in prison for a lengthy police chase that caused extensive property damage.
The chase ended abruptly when Myles stopped at a barbershop for a haircut.

Coyote Ugly

A frightened woman approached a construction worker and asked him to call the police because she saw a coyote in a Sarnia, Ontario, park while she was jogging. The woman claimed the animal had "barked" at her and she was afraid that it might chase her if she got any closer to it. The construction worker obliged. Soon police were at the location and quickly surrounded the coyote. According to a March 31, 2009, Canadian Press article, the coyote didn't move when officers arrived because it couldn't: It was a cardboard cutout, one of two that the city had installed to scare off Canada geese because they were pooping in the park. 🍁

Up in Smoke

An unnamed New Minas, Nova Scotia, man put gasoline into two containers. He didn't have a lid for one but decided to load them into his vehicle's trunk anyway. He soon noticed the smell of gasoline fumes and pulled over to make sure the uncapped container hadn't spilled. But according to a March 27, 2009, article in the *Kentville Advertiser*, as soon as he got out of his car, the man decided to have a cigarette. The resulting explosion destroyed the man's automobile, but, fortunately, said New Minas fire chief James Redmond, the driver escaped with just "a few singed hairs on his head." Just more proof that smoking is bad for your health. ✤

The First Rule of Fight Club Is You Do Not Talk About Fight Club

Police in Kingston, Ontario, responded to a man who called to report that he had been mugged and attacked by two men on his way to work. When police arrived they noticed the man "had a very swollen lip, a bloody nose, [and] maybe a broken nose," a police spokesman noted. Officers scoured the area and even brought in tracking dogs to locate the culprits, but they came up empty-handed.

After repeated questioning the police found discrepancies in the man's story, and he finally told them the truth. According to a February 8, 2009, article in the *Kingston Whig-Standard*, the man didn't want to go to work that day so he had punched himself in the face several times and called the cops. His wish did come true; he didn't go to work that day. "He got to spend most of the day in the cells under arrest for his false report," a police spokesperson said. 🍁

What a Nightmare

According to an October 7, 2008, *Edmonton Sun* article, a man filed a lawsuit in Selkirk, Manitoba, against a woman after she sued him for child support. The man's suit claims mental distress and stated that he was asleep during the 2006 encounter that led to the woman's pregnancy, and that when he woke up he demanded she "cease and desist" having sex with him, which she did. 🍁

CBC chairman Guy Fournier resigned in September 2006 after giving an interview to a French magazine in which he expounded on, as a September 20, 2006, *Toronto Star* article phrased it, "the joys of bowel movements."

Worse Than the Bundy Family

An ambulance crew was dispatched to the Toronto home of Sajid Rhatti after a 911 call about a domestic dispute with injuries was called in. When paramedics arrived they treated the twenty-three-year-old man for a broken arm and shoulder and various other wounds. The woman suffered from knife wounds to her chest, back, and legs. The two were watching *Married with Children* when they began arguing over who was prettier—Katey Sagal, who plays Peg Bundy, or Christina Applegate, who plays her daughter, Kelly.

According to a March 18, 1994, article in the *Edmonton Journal,* the argument escalated, and the wife slashed Rhatti in the groin with a wine bottle. Things settled down after that; the wife treated her husband's wounds and they sat down to continue watching the show. Minutes later, the argument flared up again. Rhatti stabbed his wife in the chest, back, and legs and suffered a broken arm and shoulder during the scuffle. After the violent episode they begged neighbors to call 911 for them. Al Bundy would have been proud. 🍁

Stick a Fork in Him: He's Done

J ason Viles had just adjusted his goggles and settled into a high-intensity Leonardo 360 tanning bed at the Millennium Tanning salon in Regina, Saskatchewan, when he suddenly noticed it was on fire. "I couldn't kick it open. I had to knock the stereo off the wall and crawl out of the back," he said. He struggled for about a minute, trying to squeeze through the narrow opening. "Anyone bigger wouldn't have gotten out." Viles was unharmed, but the business was gutted. Fire officials estimated the damage at around $300,000, according to a January 23, 2009, CBC News report. 🍁

Very Special Delivery

Rodney and Juanita Annis of Nictaux, Nova Scotia, a town so small that it isn't even listed in the census by Statistics Canada, have always joked that they're backwoods rednecks. So when Juanita's sister sent out a Facebook message requesting addresses so she could send Christmas cards, Juanita replied with "1 tree past the squirrel's hole, 3 runs past the deer lick, 1 leap over the felled oak tree."

The Christmas card, mailed from the United States, was addressed to "Hick in the Woods" at that address and, according to a January 1, 2009, Canadian Press article, was successfully delivered. "With Canada Post, everything's possible," a spokeswoman said. "The impossible sometimes, too." 🍁

On August 30, 1995, Canadian Sean Shannon recited Hamlet's "To be or not to be" soliloquy in 23.8 seconds—an average of 655 words a minute.

Oh, Pooh!

Winnie-the-Pooh, the "bear of very little brain," was named after the city of Winnipeg. Winnipeg, or Winnie, was an actual bear cub donated to the London Zoo in December 1914 by Captain Harry Colebourn and was named after the captain's hometown. Two visitors to the zoo were A. A. Milne and his son, Christopher Robin, who fell in love with the bear. Milne named his two timeless characters Christopher Robin, after his son, and Winnie-the-Pooh, after Winnipeg the bear. ✲

According to the police blotter from the
November 29, 2001, edition of the *Ottawa Sun,*
"Arrested for robbery in Ottawa: Mr. Emmanuel Innocent."

A Squeaky Clean Robbery

A man in Edmonton was approached by a knife-wielding robber who demanded all of his money. The man decided to run for it and headed to the closest lighted place, a local gas station. In order to protect himself from the pursuing robber, the man grabbed the only weapon he could find—a squeegee. The robber put away his knife, grabbed two squeegees, and chased the man around the gas station until a witness called police. According to a December 2, 2008, article in the *Edmonton Sun,* twenty-five-year-old Ryan Anthony Gambler was charged with robbery and two counts of possessing an offensive weapon [the knife, not the squeegees]. ✤

A Discriminating Disease

Since 1964, the fund-raising event Shinerama has raised more than $19.5 million to support the fight against cystic fibrosis. But in 2008, the Students' Association at Carleton University in Ottawa, which has contributed more than $1 million to Shinerama over the years, voted 17–2 to end their participation because "Cystic fibrosis has been recently revealed to only affect white people, and primarily men."

It's true that the disease does predominantly affect Caucasians, which includes indigenous populations of Europe, North Africa, the Horn of Africa, West Asia, Central Asia, and South Asia. But according to the Cystic Fibrosis Foundation, more than 70 percent of patients are diagnosed by age two, and the disease affects males and females equally. I guess these students don't know s*&t from Shinerama. 🍁

I'll Huff and Puff . . .

Police discovered thirty-four-year-old Christopher Sandberg sitting in his truck in Regina, Saskatchewan, with a canister of propane. Sandberg is known to police as a "huffer"—someone who inhales gases or chemicals to get high. While police were talking with Sandberg he decided to light up a cigarette. The resulting explosion threw both officers to the ground, and Sandberg suffered second-degree burns over more than 10 percent of his body.

According to a September 2009 article in the *Regina Leader-Post*, Sandberg was released on the condition that he not possess any pressurized substances. He was later found passed out in a park next to a propane canister and was sentenced to fourteen months in jail. ✿

Night Vision

Saskatoon, Saskatchewan, resident Stephen Townsend bravely dashed over to his neighbor's burning house at 3 a.m., kicked through a window, and rescued all six people inside. Even though his actions were heroic, Townsend doesn't take the credit for saving the lives of his neighbors [and three dogs and a cat]; he credits his common-law partner, April Knight. She was the one who woke up early and noticed the blaze and alerted the sleeping Townsend. When asked why she was up at such an early hour, Knight said she just had to go to the bathroom. So maybe it was ES-pee. 🍁

According to an August 27, 2003, CBC report, Canada's foreign ministry announced that, for "security" reasons, it would no longer issue passports if an applicant is smiling in the photo.

The Skin of Your Teeth

According to February 1995 police reports, a family in Edmonton was involved in an accident when the father, who was driving the car, temporarily lost consciousness, collided with another car, and then smashed into a utility pole. The occupants of both cars emerged relatively unscathed. Police learned that the father had become woozy and passed out after listening to his twenty-two-year-old son describe in gory detail the extraction of his wisdom teeth earlier in the day. 🍁

Not a Bunch of Bologna

In September 2008, responding to reports of an outbreak of listeriosis, a dangerous bacterial infection that, in this incident, was caused by contaminated sandwich meats, Gerry Ritz, Canada's federal agriculture minister, was heard saying, "This is like a death by a thousand cuts. Or should I say 'cold cuts'?" Ritz made the comment while on a conference call updating scientists and bureaucrats on the outbreak.

When Ritz was informed of yet another death [the disease eventually claimed seventeen lives], this time on Prince Edward Island, he replied, "Please tell me it's [Liberal MP] Wayne Easter." Ritz apologized for his gallows humor, saying the outbursts were made during "a highly stressful time." He admitted his jokes "were tasteless and completely inappropriate." What do you expect from a wisecracker like Ritz? ✤

Sweet Surrender

After the school board in Burnaby, British Columbia, east of Vancouver, ruled that school sales of chocolate bars and other candies and sugary treats were forbidden, a group of entrepreneurial students created a lucrative black market. Three unnamed high school students told the Canadian Broadcasting Corporation that they racked in about $200 a week selling contraband sweets. One student even bragged that he advertised his inventory on Facebook.

Burnaby Board of Education chairwoman Kathy Corrigan said the students weren't going to get busted by the board. "We are not going to come down hard on these students," she said. "I have to admire their entrepreneurial spirit." 🍁

According to an
October 14, 2008, CBC
News report, while visiting
his parents' gravesite at the
Saint Gregoire Cemetery
in Buckingham, Quebec, a
seventy-seven-year-old man
was crushed to death when a
tombstone fell on him.

A Pet Peeve

Frances Woodard suffers from agoraphobia and is under doctor's orders to travel with a companion animal to comfort her during her trips on Ottawa's transit system. She has fought with the Canadian Transportation Agency about her companion animal and has had to file complaints to the OC Transpo transit agency.

The main complaint isn't that Woodard has a companion animal; it's that the companion animal is a ferret. Eventually she was granted special privileges to travel with Gyno [pronounced "Jeeno"], but no one else is allowed to travel with a pet, caged or not, except for Seeing Eye dogs. 🍁

A Costumed Crusader

Captain Scotty," part of the morning crew at radio station CFOX in Vancouver, set out to prove just how easy it is to buy drugs in the city. He donned a beaver costume with a sign proclaiming that he was in the market to buy some heroin, went down to the city's Downtown Eastside neighborhood, and within minutes the transaction was completed.

The entire episode was broadcast live on *The Jeff O'Neil Show,* which included in its listening audience two police officers in the area. When they went to the location, the dealer was nowhere to be found, but they easily spotted the oversized beaver. "They found him, intervened, and took a small amount of heroin from him," a police spokeswoman said. 🍁

Slurpeetoba

Without the need for a straw poll, on July 10, 2009, Winnipeg was once again named 7-Eleven's Slurpee capital of the world, marking a full decade at the top of the Slurpee chain. How serious is Winnipeg when it comes to Slurpee consumption? "A lot of the stores in Winnipeg have brides and grooms that go in on their wedding days and get photos done with Slurpees. It's that ingrained in the culture there," noted 7-Eleven spokeswoman Sheila Calder. "And apparently, the Slurpee is the number one beverage served to women in Winnipeg maternity wards." 🍁

What's in a Name?

Police in Regina, Saskatchewan, armed with an arrest warrant, knocked on the door of a house belonging to twenty-eight-year-old David William McKay. A man matching McKay's description opened the door but adamantly stated he wasn't McKay. He claimed his name was Matthew but was unable to spell it, and he said he knew McKay and that he was "a badass."

When "Matthew," who wasn't wearing a shirt, turned around, police noticed the name "David McKay" tattooed on his back. The man still insisted he wasn't David McKay, but police arrested him anyway. Turns out, the man was David McKay, and he was sentenced to forty-five days for obstruction of police. ✤

Hurling the Law

City councillors in Windsor, Ontario, are sick and tired of people being sick on their city streets and have proposed an "antifouling" bylaw making vomiting in public a finable offense. The proposal would also make public urination and littering finable offenses as well, and force hot dog vendors to close up at 2 a.m. and after-hours clubs to close by 3 a.m. In an April 28, 2008, UPI article, Remo Agostino, owner of the Boom Boom Room nightclub, was quoted as saying, "How are you going to stop someone from throwing up?" 🍁

Betcha didn't know that Sir Sandford Fleming, who designed Canada's first stamp, also devised time zones in February 1879.

You Took the Words
Right Out of My Mouth

The Canadian Broadcasting Corporation reported on March 8, 2006, that students at Mount Saint Vincent University in Bedford, Nova Scotia, had successfully petitioned the administration to disallow professors from using any plagiarism-detecting aid, because it fosters, according to the student union president, a "culture of mistrust." 🍁

The CBC News reported
on April 18, 2001, that a
Vancouver apartment complex
was evacuated and condemned
after a dentist died inhaling
toxic vapors. For reasons
unknown, the dentist had
amassed a large quantity of
mercury that he routinely
played with.

Eating Like a Pig

Researchers at the University of Guelph in Ontario reported in 2001 that they had developed Enviropig, a new breed of Yorkshire pig that uses plant phosphorus more efficiently. The genetically enhanced porkers are able to more effectively digest phytate, a phosphate found in their cereal grain diet, thereby eliminating the farmer's need to supplement the pig's diet with phosphate or phytase enzymes. Farmers traditionally include phosphate in pig slop to foster optimal growth and development. 🍁

A Negative Effect

Three teenagers, a boy and two girls, entered Tony's Old Time Portrait Studio in Victoria, British Columbia, to have their pictures taken while wearing period costumes provided by the studio. The staff spent forty-minutes with the three youths getting them into costumes, arranging the set, and taking the photographs. The kids took a look at the finished product and then "took off like a bat out of hell" without paying their eighty-four-dollar sitting fee, owner Tony Bohanan said.

Bohanan didn't wait to see what would develop; he decided to release the portraits and ask the public for help in tracking down the film-flamming felons. As soon as the photos hit the media all three of the teens turned themselves in. "We saw our pictures plastered all over the place and it made me feel like a crook," one of the girls said. ❦

Reach Out
and Touch Someone

The phone at a convenience store in Windsor, Ontario, rang and the clerk answered it. The caller on the other line asked a question the clerk had never heard before. "[The person] called up and asked how much money was in the till," said police detective Al Thompson. Sure enough, "Not quite an hour and a half later, he came in and robbed the place." Forty-year-old Daniel Glen was immediately arrested on robbery charges. Although Thompson called the case "pretty unusual," he noted that Glen is suspected in two other unsolved robberies; both times the robber called the store in advance. 🍁

In January 2000, a Canadian MP released a list of pamphlets directly funded by the government, including "How to Communicate with the Dead," "How to Stimulate the G-spot," and "How to Understand and Enjoy an Orgasm."

A Double-Edged Proposal

I was shocked. It just happened so fast that I just grabbed the ring, put it on, and hugged and kissed him," said Michelle Taitt of the unexpected marriage proposal. What was more unexpected was the fact that her fiancé, John Rossall, proposed to her in a Scarborough, Ontario, courtroom right after she had been acquitted of threatening him with a knife.

During the trial, Rossall admitted he had given a false report to the police and that Taitt had never brandished a knife against him. "I loved him from the first blind date," Taitt told the *Toronto Sun* in a February 23, 2006, article. ✿

Mass Appeal

According to a December 30, 2005, *Globe and Mail* article, the latest snack craze to hit Quebec is Communion wafers. "My son can eat a whole bag while he's watching TV," said one man. "They melt in your mouth, and they're not fattening," said one woman. But not everyone is happy about the snacking on the host with the most. "They're not distinguishing between the body of Christ and something you nibble on at home," complained a former Catholic missionary. No word on whether they go well with wine. 🍁

In October 1999, in the village of Tracadie Cross, Prince Edward Island, the driver of a hearse lost control of the vehicle and ran over and killed a sixty-eight-year-old pallbearer who had just left a funeral.

Slow-Speed Chase

A call came into a Toronto police department warning officers that a man driving a backhoe was heading toward a car wash, apparently with the intention of knocking down a portion of the wall in order to get at the facilities coin machine. The call came in from a vehicle that had left its intended route in order to chase the would-be robber.

According to a February 13, 2008, article in the *Toronto Star*, the vehicle that was pursuing the backhoe was . . . a snowplow. 🍁

Hit the Hershey Highway

In order to get off welfare, forty-seven-year-old Guy Masse took a job at a Zellers department store in Saint-Hyacinthe, Quebec, for just a couple of months in 2005. Just before Christmas, Masse discovered a number of discarded chocolate bars in the trash Dumpster and thought he would take them and give them to his children. Even though the candy bars had been thrown away, they were technically still store property and Masse was fired.

"Unfortunately, this associate breached the trust of his supervisors by removing merchandise from the store, and as a result, he was let go from his position," said Hillary Stauth, spokeswoman for the Hudson's Bay Company, which owns the store chain. 🍁

Smile, You're on Candid Camera

Donovan James Clements called police in Moncton, New Brunswick, claiming he had been accosted by four men who robbed him of the bottle of whiskey he had just purchased from a liquor store. Officers went into the liquor store and asked the owner if they could review the store's security camera tapes in hopes of identifying the four men. Much to their amusement, the tape never showed the four alleged men but, according to an October 18, 2005, article in the *Moncton Times and Transcript*, it did show Clements stealing the bottle of whiskey. Clements was arrested for theft and was sentenced to two years of probation. ✹

In January 2005, police in Edmonton investigated a man selling "guaranteed admission into heaven" for twenty dollars. The man's Web site claims, "[It works without] need for confessions or penance."

Who Moved My Cheese?

L uc Boivin, a cheese maker from Quebec, wanted to test his theory that cheese would taste better if ripened in cold, deep water. So Boivin dropped 800 kilograms [1,764 pounds] of cheddar into La Baie des Ha! Ha!, a fjord in Saguenay, Quebec, and waited. When he went back to see if his theory was valid, he couldn't find his cheese.

According to a July 30, 2005, *Globe and Mail* article, Boivin finally gave up after spending $50,000 on scuba divers and sonar equipment looking for his lost wheel of cheese. 🍁

Hey, I've Got an Idea

Rosaire Roy of Prince Albert, Saskatchewan, pleaded guilty in 2002 to hiring Tracy Bannab to fulfill a sexual fantasy. But it's not as simple as it sounds. Roy hired Bannab to enter his store, armed with a pellet gun, and force him and a female acquaintance to remove their clothes and assume a sexual position. She then tied them together, took the money from the till, and made her escape.

The female was able to untie her bonds, free Roy, and call the police. Crown prosecutor John Syrnick did not charge Bannab because she obviously didn't realize that Roy's female acquaintance wasn't in on the plan. 🍁

On September 22, 2003, Reuters reported that
Canadian military police seized 983 marijuana plants
in Nicolet, Quebec, that squatters were growing on an
active seventeen-square-mile artillery range.

Things That Go Bump in the Night

Donald Johnson, a defense attorney in Cornwall, Ontario, was awakened in the middle of the night by noises coming from another bedroom in his house. His wife called police while Johnson went in search of the intruder. He jumped the burglar and struggled with him, finally disarming him of his knife. He rolled him over and got a good look at the man: It was one of his clients.

"I guess he didn't know it was my house," Johnson said. During his booking, police asked thirty-four-year-old Scott Best if he'd like to call a lawyer, and he asked if he could call Johnson. He was persuaded to call a different attorney. According to a May 28, 2005, article in the *Ottawa Citizen,* Johnson agreed with the officer's suggestion; it "wouldn't have been a good idea" to call him, he said. 🍁

Please Hang Up
and Try Again

Chester Gillan, the health minister for Prince Edward Island, announced in May 2005 a novel way of saving tax money: Reduce the hours of operation of the provincial suicide prevention hotline from twenty-four hours a day to normal business hours: 9 a.m. to 5 p.m. Gillan's rationale was that the hotline had received only fifty calls from suicidal people the previous year at a taxpayers' cost of $30,000. After a public outcry and complaints from the Canadian Association for Suicide Prevention, Gillan rescinded his proposal. 🍁

After Britain conquered Quebec in 1759, it offered to trade it back in exchange for Guadeloupe. France refused.

The Wrong Kind of Stick Up

A teenager in Toronto approached a woman in a store parking lot, waved a knife in her face, and ordered her out of her car. He quickly jumped in the car and started it up but then had a change of heart. It wasn't that he felt sorry for the woman; it was that the idiot didn't know how to drive a manual stick shift. After several lurching, failed attempts, he asked a passerby to drive the car, but the person refused. The disgruntled teen was captured later that day attempting to carjack yet another vehicle. 🍁

Emergency operators in Peterborough, Ontario, received a 911 call at 3 a.m. from a man asking if they would give him a wake-up call in the morning. The operator reminded the man that 911 was for emergencies only, but minutes later he called back again requesting the same wake-up call. His number was traced, and Donald Archie Baker, who had an outstanding warrant for theft, was arrested at his home.

Float Like a Butterfly

The idea was simple: jump off the Canada Trust Bank Building in Calgary, Alberta, on April 1, 2005, with a parachute strapped to his back and float safely to the ground. But what forty-one-year-old Scott Watwood didn't take into consideration was a potential shift in the winds—which caused him to slam into a twenty-fourth-floor window. The window broke, and the shattered glass then smashed through seven windows in the atrium below. Watwood was taken to a hospital suffering from pelvic, back, and abdominal injuries. To add insult to his injuries he was found guilty of mischief and fined $1,500. 🍁

A Slap on the Wrist

Winnipeg judge Charles Rubin caused quite a stir in his courtroom after he acquitted an alleged mugger and then chastised his victim. Apparently, the forty-six-year-old victim was walking down the street holding money in his hands shortly before he was accosted.

"We have a very stupid civilian who admits that he was stupid," said Judge Rubin, who, according to a July 20, 2000, article in the *Winnipeg Free Press,* interrupted the Crown's closing summation to deliver his verdict. "If you walk around jingling money in your hand . . . it's like walking in the wolf enclosure at the city zoo with a pound of ground beef in your hand. And it's almost the same type of predators you're going to find out there."

The judge also advised the complainant that, in the future, he should consider walking in the middle of the street instead of on the sidewalk. The victim told the newspaper that he was insulted by the judge's comments and that his lawyer is considering an appeal. 🍁

Fire One! Fire Two!

George Pavlovsky, a senior tree cutter for the city of Moncton, New Brunswick, showed up to work intoxicated and carrying a loaded sawed-off shotgun in a quest to find his two supervisors, who had recently passed him up for promotion. Colleagues fled in fear as the enraged Pavlovsky stomped through the halls wielding his shotgun. As a result, according to a November 28, 2003, article in the *Globe and Mail,* Pavlovsky was fired from his job in April 2003, arrested, and sentenced to two years in jail.

But a short seven days later, Canadian Union of Public Employees Local 51 filed a motion to get Pavlovsky his job back when he gets out of prison. Several of Pavlovsky's colleagues who witnessed his rampage were still on stress leave at the time. 🍁

Freedom in Prison

In a June 7, 2002, article in the *National Post*, the Correctional Service of Canada heralded new successful model programs in several prisons. One of the programs allowed inmates who requested it to reside in specific wings of the prison designated as "drug-free zones"—even though it's a hard and fast rule that all sections of the prison are required to be free of drugs. 🍁

The CBC reported on August 16, 2007, that an arbitrator had ordered the largest school district in Montreal to rehire a teacher it had fired in 2004. The school had released the teacher for failing to disclose a conviction for murdering his wife, but the arbitrator ruled that his previous actions were unrelated to his ability to function as a teacher.

Hit and Run with the Money

Robert Daniel Irving was deemed eligible by the Manitoba Public Insurance fund to collect $30,000 in standard spousal death benefits after his wife died in an automobile accident. It was assumed by many that Irving would be denied his claim based on the fact that his wife was a passenger in his car at the time, and he was driving while intoxicated. Irving pleaded guilty to impaired driving, but according to a May 10, 2002, article in the *Sault Star*, the insurance agency stated that his plea was immaterial concerning his eligibility for benefits. ❧

Ill Will

Judge Gerald Jewers of the Manitoba Court of Queen's Bench awarded fifty-five-year-old Lynette Mary Sant $66,000 because chemical vapors from a local company had made her ill. The judge issued his ruling even though there was no evidence that the vapors had anything to do with Sant's illness. In fact, according to an April 26, 2002, article in the *National Post,* tests conducted on Sant using distilled water had the identical effect. 🍁

The *National Post* reported on October 1, 2008, that Muri Chilton (aka Murray Gartton), who is serving a life sentence for the rape and murder of a fifteen-year-old girl, was awarded $2,500 by a Canadian federal court judge. Chilton argued that he should be compensated because he felt "utterly humiliated" in 2000 when guards laughed at him after he injured his thumb in a prison workshop accident.

You're in My Urine

Canadian military officials told reporters in September 1999 that twenty-three of their thirty-two Hercules transport aircraft required expensive structural repairs to replace the main aluminum beams. The beams had become corroded by uric acid from soldiers' urine that had splashed on the beams or because they had completely missed the crude toilets in the planes' cargo holds. 🍁

Where Are We Now?

In 2001, the Canadian Tourism Commission was embarrassed to find out that a travel guide they had contracted left out a few things. Those few minor oversights were Prince Edward Island; the Yukon; Halifax, Nova Scotia; Fredericton, New Brunswick; and Brandon, Manitoba. The brochure also referred to "Newfoundland and Labrador" as simply "Newfoundland" [even though its official title had changed two years earlier], and Nunavut was misspelled. Fodor's Travel Guides, a U.S. company, was paid $600,000 to produce the guide. A commission spokesman said their relationship with that company is under review. 🍁

Paint-Skating Endeavor

A dministrators of the Shaw Millennium skateboard park in Calgary, Alberta, thought it would be a good idea, and generate some free publicity, if they opened up their park to anyone who wanted to spruce up its bare walls with art. "Young urban artists will have a chance to show off their work to their peers and influence the recreational space they use," said the press release issued by the city.

The city administrators provided the paint and believed the process would take up to three months to complete. But they were completely surprised when after only two days the entire park was covered in paint, including the insides of the restrooms. "They destroyed the fricking park," said Alderman John Mar. "They graffitied the hell out of it. They tagged the entire fricking park!" According to an August 27, 2009, article in the *Calgary Sun,* the cost of the cleanup will be between $30,000 and $60,000. A local who witnessed the paint-a-thon said, "No one was watching or supervising. What did they think would happen?" ❧

Fake Plastic

In July 2007, a clerk at an Edmonton shopping center was presented with an obviously fake credit card and asked the owner to provide identification, which he did. The clerk confiscated several other fake credit cards from the customer and notified the police.

As police were beginning their investigation they received another call; a man had stopped by police headquarters to complain about confiscated credit cards. They quickly put two and two together, raided two hotel rooms, and rounded up two more suspects in an identity theft ring. They also netted dozens of other fake credit cards, equipment to make them, and thousands of dollars in cash. The main counterfeiter, Eric Stephens, was sentenced to sixteen months in a provincial jail while charges against his two accomplices were withdrawn. 🍁

A Working-Class Hero

In December 2003, Yves Julien worked an eleven-hour shift, plus overtime, for the Canada Border Services Agency, and then requested to be reimbursed nine dollars for a sandwich he had purchased when asked to put in the extra hours. The agency refused his request, claiming that his contract with them disallowed reimbursement for foodstuffs because he was already earning premium pay for the hours he put in.

According to a September 10, 2008, article in the *Globe and Mail*, Julien sued, and nearly five years after the incident, he was awarded his nine dollars. ❦

Lawyer Christian Gauthier faced a disciplinary investigation after his actions during a trial break at a Montreal courthouse. According to a November 4, 2003, CBC News report, Gauthier was defending a client accused of killing a police officer when he was overheard singing the Bob Marley song "I Shot the Sheriff."

That Guy Is a Real Boob

Tommy's is offering to you the chance of a lifetime. You have a shot at winning BOOBS. That is right, you did read correctly." The September 2000 contest at Tommy's Bar and Grill in Maple Ridge, British Columbia, offered $3,000 breast implants to the winner. According to restaurant manager Melina Vince, more than three thousand entries were tallied, and not all of them came from women. Apparently the fine print didn't specify the type of plastic surgery the winner would receive. ✦

There Goes the Neighborhood

A ccording to a November 13, 2002, Canadian Press article, the town of Colwood, British Columbia, enlisted the services of a retired professor to find out why TVs and VCRs were starting automatically, sprinklers were coming on, automatic garage doors were opening suddenly, and one couple's mechanical bed had folded up while they were asleep. The primary suspects were two broadcast transmission towers that had been recently installed. 🍁

An August 2, 2006, article in the *Toronto Star* told the story of Marty Descoteaux, who jumped out of his idling boat in Elliot Lake, Ontario, after a bear climbed into it. The bear hit the throttle and took off over the lake. The boat eventually hit a rock and the bear was thrown back into the water.

Two Peas in a Pod

Two brothers, both in their fifties, were arrested and convicted of throwing onions and oranges from a nineteenth-floor balcony at local police officers who were investigating a break-in on the ground floor. The brothers, David and Daniel Dauphinee, have had previous confrontations with law-enforcement officials and are no strangers to police, according to a July 3, 2002, article in the *National Post,* as both men are retired senior members of the Royal Canadian Mounted Police. David's ex-wife Debbie described the men as "dumb and dumber." 🍁

A robber snatched the cash drawer from a convenience store in Hamilton, Ontario, and took off on foot. He was pursued by the petite clerk in her early twenties, who grabbed the money back from him. A tug-of-war ensued, which, according to a February 7, 2007, article in the *Hamilton Spectator*, the young woman won.

Service for One

The *Guardian* reported on February 9, 2002, that the Federal Court of Canada had ruled that Hugh Trainor was entitled to veterans' benefits for service during World War II. Trainor had been ruled medically unfit for the armed services and had never served a single day. It was argued, however, that his boat ride from Prince Edward Island to Nova Scotia, where the recruiting station physical exam took place, qualified as dangerous service, because, at the time, German submarines were thought to be operating in the Atlantic Ocean. ✤

Repeatedly Offended

Mark Turner was found guilty of bank robbery and served four years of an eleven-year sentence before being released from a halfway house by the National Parole Board of Canada in 1987. In 1993, Turner was arrested again for conspiracy to commit robbery and was returned to prison, but he claims it's not his fault.

"I feel the [Correctional Service of Canada] and CSC parole are responsible for my every move while under their supervision," Turner said in an affidavit filed in the Federal Court of Canada. Therefore, according to a January 2, 2002, article in the *Globe and Mail,* Turner is suing the parole board for $1.6 million because he claims he shouldn't have been released early, and had he served his entire sentence he would have been more suited for a crime-free life. 🍁

A Hard Sleep

Convicted drug trafficker Khon Ha Tri fell out of the top bunk in his prison cell in 1996 and tore a knee ligament. So he filed a lawsuit against the Peterborough, Ontario, prison claiming that, after an earlier accident, the prison doctor had informed the guards that he should sleep in a lower bunk and the guards had ignored the doctor's orders. According to a January 24, 2001, *National Post* article, Tri was released from prison after the lawsuit was filed, but a Canadian court ruled in his favor. He has since been rejailed on another charge. ✤

Too Little, Too Late

The December 5, 2000, edition of *USA Today* reported that the Transportation Safety Board of Canada had recommended that airlines reduce the amount of procedural time they spend in cross-checking after the detection of an onboard fire. This recommendation came after the board's investigation of the 1998 crash of Swissair Flight 111, in which it would have taken pilots thirty minutes to complete their checklist. Flight 111 crashed twenty minutes after the initial report of smoke. 🍁

Art for Art's Sake

In February 2000, Canada's Reform Party publicly denounced $64 million of art grants given by the Canada Council for the Arts. Among the grants were $4,200 for a video on the rubber stamp "as a low-tech marking device"; $3,200 for a documentary on chewing gum in history and culture; and $950 for a pamphlet written by an aboriginal illuminating one of his race's anatomical traits, entitled "Where Did My Ass Go?" 🍁

According to an October 12, 2002, *Globe and Mail* article, David M. Voth, of Saskatoon, Saskatchewan, who wrote a best-seller on how to escape paying income tax in Canada, was fined for his failure to file income tax returns since 1995.